MARY ENGELBREIT

HEY, KIDS! COME CRAFT WITH ME

Meredith® Press
Des Moines, Iowa

Contents

CHAPTER 1
EVERYONE NEEDS THEIR OWN SPOT

Your bedroom! Your space! Your getaway place! This chapter gives you ideas galore for cool stuff to make for your very own hideaway.

CHAPTER 2 PALS

Celebrate friendship with fun crafts! From pretty tea linens to wacky pogo sticks and paddleballs that'll make you giggle, playtime has never been more fun!

CHAPTER 3
STEPPING OUT

Make it...wear it...get ready for some "wows!" From mittens on your fingers to sneakers on your toes, you'll be the talk of the lunchroom!

CHAPTER **4**
ONE TOUCH OF NATURE

Take a hike (even if it's in your own backyard) to collect supplies for these fun nature crafts! You learn how to make stamped prints, an outdoor game board—even frames and mats to keep or give to Mom and Dad!

CHAPTER **5**
THE PRINCESS OF QUITE–A–LOT

Want to be the reigning queen of the kingdom...or at least dress the part? We'll show you how to make some great make-believe costumes—and even a trunk to store all your new fancy duds!

CHAPTER **6**
WELL, AIN'T YOU SOMETHIN'?!

Want to create something with no help at all? Here's your chance— get ready to stand tall! From pretty pasta ornaments to hang on the Christmas tree to stationery to keep in touch with a special someone, you're on your own to have lots of fun!

Making Things

Welcome to this fun book of crafts that you can make. I'm glad you've come along with me to discover the excitement of creating things yourself! I know many of you like to draw and craft. I know how you feel—I have loved drawing my whole life!

I started drawing from the time I could hold a crayon. When I was a little older my mother helped me create a tiny "artist's studio" by cramming a little desk into a cleaned out linen closet. I spent hours in my little studio just drawing away. Have you ever thought of making a space for yourself—a special little spot to call your own and to keep all of your treasured arts and crafts supplies? (It's kind of like having a secret hideaway to create things you love.)

I used to like to draw with a dipping pen. (That's a pen that you dip in a bottle of ink.) Then I would color my drawings with colored pencils. Sometimes I would draw

For Mommy on her Birthday

Love, Mary

Aa Bb Cc
Cat Bat

So that is why we have teachers...

AND THEN AGAIN SOME PEOPLE JUST PLAY WITH BOOKS (WHICH WE REALLY SHOULDN'T DO!)

PEOPLE WITH JOBS HAVE TO READ BOOKS TO KNOW WHAT TO DO.

BELOW OPPOSITE: These are some of the pictures I drew as a present for my mother when I was about ten years old.
ABOVE: When I was eleven I drew these pictures for a book called "A Little Book About Books."

pictures to go with whatever book I was reading. It was fun and it helped me become a part of the story. I guess you could say I was illustrating stories when I was ten years old! By the time I was eleven, I knew I wanted to be an artist for the rest of my life.

In high school, my classmates would ask me to draw and make all kinds of greeting cards—like birthday cards for friends. I loved it! It was fun to give them away and it gave me a lot of practice.

As I drew more and more, a local shopkeeper paid me 25 cents for each greeting card I drew for him. (He finally raised it to 50 cents.) That was a great way for me to make a little extra money and I got to draw and make things at the same time.

In this book we've shown you all kinds of things you can make from all kinds of different materials. Whether you like to draw, paint, work with clay, or just make things to keep or give as special gifts, we've filled this book with lots of projects for you to create. I know you'll love this book, and I hope it will be the beginning of even more ideas for you as you come along and craft with me.

Mary Engelbreit

EVERYONE
NEEDS THEIR OWN
SPOT

Your room is your castle, your awesome space, your secret hideaway! We've come up with some cool projects for you to make for your own special spot. Turn the page for some clever crafts—complete with instructions so you can start making fun projects right away!

EVERYONE NEEDS THEIR OWN SPOT.

· ROBERT WHALEN ·

My Own Special Chair

You'll be sittin' pretty in this adorable armchair that shows off your creativity and artistic talents.

WHAT YOU'LL NEED

- White canvas, enough to upholster a chair
- A chair just your size that can be upholstered
- Waxed paper
- Paint pens and permanent markers

OH,NO

Q I don't have a chair I can cover—what can I do?

A Lots! Just draw your favorite works of art or happy sayings on fabric and make it into a pillow or place mat. Or, you can purchase these items and simply draw away!

HERE'S HOW

1 Ask a grown-up to figure out how much canvas is needed to cover the chair. Once the fabric is purchased, lay it on a waxed-paper-covered floor.

▼**2** Draw pictures and write messages on the fabric, using paint pens and permanent markers. (You can have friends or family members help you if you want.) Let the paint and marker dry.

3 Ask a grown-up to take the fabric and the chair to an upholstery shop. The upholsterer will cover the chair with the unique fabric you have created.

Secret Diary Cover

Keep all of your thoughts and dreams locked up tightly in this blooming diary you can make and share with your best friend (only if you want to).

WHAT YOU'LL NEED

- Waxed paper
- Purchased diary with lock and key
- Acrylic paints in leaf green, pink, yellow, red, and white
- Paintbrush
- Crayola® Model Magic lightweight modeling compound
- Rolling pin
- Round and flower-shaped cookie cutters
- Thick white crafts glue
- Silver permanent marker
- Black permanent marker

HERE'S HOW

▲**1** Cover work surface with waxed paper. Open the diary and lay it with the cover side up. Paint it with green paint. Let it dry. Paint it again if necessary.

2 Tear off two pieces of waxed paper. Place a handful of Model Magic between the sheets of waxed paper. Use a rolling pin to roll the Model Magic until it is about ¼-inch thick. Remove the top sheet.

▲**3** Using cookie cutters, cut out flowers using the photograph, *opposite*, as a guide. To make round flowers, cut two sizes of circles for each flower. To make leaves, first cut a circle. Using the same cookie cutter, cut the circle in half. The result will be a leaf shape. Let the shapes dry for 24 hours.

4 Paint the flowers as you wish. Mix a little white paint with green to paint the leaves. Let the paint dry. Glue the layered flowers together. Add white highlights to the flowers.

▲**5** Arrange the painted shapes on the cover of the diary. Glue the shapes in place. Let the glue dry.

6 Write your name and the word "diary" on one of the leaves with markers.

▲**7** To make polka dots, dip the tip of the paintbrush handle into white paint and dab it on the areas around the flowers and leaves. Let the paint dry.

OH, NO

Q I don't have any Model Magic and I want to decorate my diary right now. Can you help?

A You can make similar flowers by tracing cookie-cutter shapes onto felt or fun foam. Then cut them out and glue them onto your diary.

Autograph Lampshade

Let friendship shine by asking your best buddies to help you create this extra-special lampshade.

WHAT YOU'LL NEED

- Fabric paint pens in bright pink, white, black, royal blue, sky blue, and iridescent white glitter
- Paper plate
- Paintbrush
- Lamp with fabric shade

HERE'S HOW

1 Squeeze pink paint onto a paper plate. Using a paintbrush, paint the lampshade. If there is binding at the top or the bottom of the shade, paint it white. Let the paint dry.

2 Using paint pens, have friends sign their names on the pink area of the shade. Let the paint dry.

▲ **3** Fill in blank areas of the shade by drawing daisy shapes with white paint pen. Once dry, fill in the flowers if you wish.

▼ **4** With a royal blue paint pen, make dots or checks on the areas that are painted white. Let the paint dry. If painting checks, add dots to the centers of the checks if you wish.

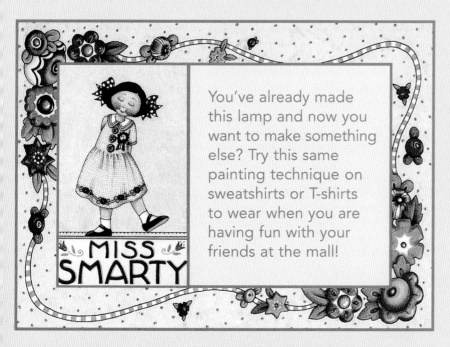

MISS SMARTY

You've already made this lamp and now you want to make something else? Try this same painting technique on sweatshirts or T-shirts to wear when you are having fun with your friends at the mall!

Telephone Message Mat

Make a fresh-from-the-garden mat for your dresser top by cutting simple shapes out of sponge rubber mats and sewing them onto the background with shoelaces.

WHAT YOU'LL NEED	•Tracing paper •Pencil; scissors •Woven sponge rubber place	mats or by-the-roll sponge rubber in green and	other bright colors (you can buy this at discount stores)	•45-inch-long green and white shoelaces •Coffee cup

HERE'S HOW

▲**1** Place tracing paper over the leaf pattern and trace the leaf shape. Cut it out. Trace around the leaf pattern on the green sponge rubber and cut it out. Repeat to make as many leaf shapes as you like. Set the leaves aside.

2 If using sponge rubber on a roll, cut a background piece into a shape you like. Otherwise, use the place mat.

▲**3** Decide where you want to add a flower to your mat. Using a green shoelace, insert an end into the open weave of the mat (where you would like the top of the stem) and bring the end back through the hole just below the first one. Using the long end of the shoelace, bring it straight down and insert the end of the lace about 1 inch from the bottom edge of the mat.

▲**4** Decide where you want your leaves. Poke the end of the lace up through one of the leaves, as close to the stem as possible. Sew on the leaf by poking the lace end through the layers of rubber near the tip of the leaf. Do this to sew on all the leaves.

5 Cut a circle from sponge rubber, using a coffee cup to trace the circle.

6 Using a white shoelace, sew on the flower using large stitches to create an "X."

7 For a woven edge, weave laces at the top and bottom of the mat. Trim the lace ends.

OH.NO

Q I can't find sponge rubber place mats or woven sponge rubber on a roll. What can I use?

A You also can make these mats using colored plastic canvas found in the needlework section of crafts shops or discount stores.

LEAF PATTERN

Fairest-of-all Mirror Set

Pretend you're a princess
or the queen herself when
you look into this magical
mirror decorated
with swirling
colors of yarn.

WHAT YOU'LL NEED

• Thick white crafts glue
• Handheld mirror, brush, and comb
  set with smooth, flat surfaces
• Paintbrush
• Scissors
• Yarns in your favorite colors
• Jewels

HERE'S HOW

▲**1** Apply a few dabs of glue on the top of the mirror handle and smear it around with your finger or a paintbrush.

▲**2** Beginning at the top of the handle, place the yarn on the glue and start winding the yarn around until the entire handle is covered; add glue as you go. You can use one color of yarn or several different colors.

3 Cover the back of the mirror with a thin layer of glue and wind the yarn on the glued area.

▲**4** You can wind yarn in any shapes you like. Keep adding colors around the shapes until the whole area is covered. Add jewels with glue.

5 Decorate the brush and the comb using the same yarn and jewel techniques.

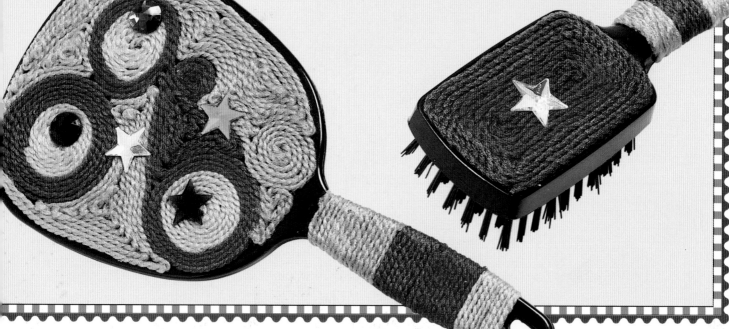

Store-Your-Stuff Crates

Tidy up your room and keep
it that way with the help of
these easy-to-decorate miniature
storage crates.

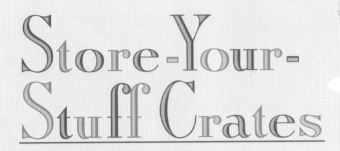

WHAT YOU'LL NEED

- Plastic or wire mesh crates
- Ribbons; scissors; tape and beads (optional)

HERE'S HOW

◄ **2** Tie a bow and trim the ribbon ends.

▲ **1** To weave a small crate with ribbon, decide where you want the bow. Start weaving the ribbon there. Weave ribbon in and out in an "over-one, under-one" manner until the ribbon ends meet or are close together.

3 To add beads, cut ribbon pieces to go around the crate, adding about 8 inches. To make it easy to add beads, wind tape around one end of each ribbon piece (like on a shoelace). Weave the ribbons, adding beads as desired. Tie the ribbon ends together on the inside. ◄

MISS SMARTY

Is this too easy? Try making patterns like Xs or weave the ribbon diagonally. You also can thread buttons with shanks onto your ribbon or mix colors of ribbons to make your crates really cute!

Show-off Bulletin Board

Create a place to tuck
(or tack) all of your important
messages, clippings, school
pictures, and more!

WHAT YOU'LL NEED

- 12x12-inch piece of 1-inch-thick Styrofoam®
- 16x16-inch piece of yellow felt
- White crafts glue

- 8 yellow straight pins, plus 16 additional pins in any color
- Scissors

- About 2 yards of ¼-inch-wide turquoise satin ribbon
- Tracing paper

- 8x8-inch piece of white felt
- Four 1½-inch daisy appliqués

CORNER BOW PATTERN

HERE'S HOW

▲**1** Center the Styrofoam on top of the yellow felt. Fold the felt edges to the back and glue them in place, letting the corners stick out. If the felt won't stay in place while the glue is drying, use a pin to hold it. Let the glue dry.

▲**2** Cut four 16-inch-long pieces of ribbon. Lay the ribbons across the front of the bulletin board, approximately 2 inches from the edges. Using the yellow straight pins, pin each ribbon end on the outside edge of the bulletin board.

▲**3** Turn the bulletin board to the back. Glue and pin the ribbon ends to the back of the Styrofoam. Be sure the pins do not stick through the front of the bulletin board. Let the glue dry.

▼**4** Knot the ends of the remaining piece of ribbon.

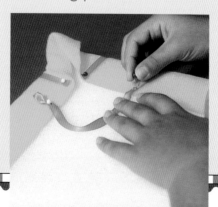

With one corner of the bulletin board at the top, pin the knotted ribbon about 4 inches down from each side to make a hanger.

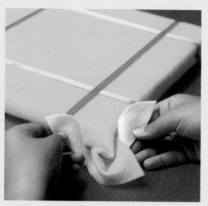

▲**5** Trace the bow pattern, *opposite*, onto the tracing paper and cut out the pattern. Trace around the pattern onto the white felt four times. Cut out the bows. Tie the white bows onto the yellow felt corners of the bulletin board.

6 Glue the daisy appliqués in the corners of the bulletin board. Let the glue dry.

PALS

It's always fun to make the stuff you play with—and even more fun to share it with a pal! In this chapter you'll find all kinds of great things to make and to play with too. From bouncing yo-yos to pogo sticks that really go—turn the page for some playtime favorites for you and your special friends!

Snazzy Yos

You'll be the talk around the world (and among your pals) with your own decorated yo-yo to show your stuff.

WHAT YOU'LL NEED

- Waxed paper; old or new yo-yo
- Acrylic paints in colors you like
- Paintbrushes
- Thick white crafts glue
- Beads, jewels, or flower shapes cut from lace pieces

HERE'S HOW

1 Cover your work surface with waxed paper. Paint one side of the yo-yo. (You don't need to paint the inside by the string.) Let it dry.

2 Turn the yo-yo over and paint the other side. Let that side dry. Give each side another coat of paint. Let both sides dry thoroughly.

▲ **3** To paint the dots on the yo-yo like our black one, use the handle of your paintbrush dipped in the paint.

4 Glue beads, jewels, or shapes cut from lace pieces onto your yo-yo.

OH, NO

Q What if I paint my yo-yo and then wish I had painted it differently?

A The great thing about acrylic paint is that, after it dries, you can paint over it again. It may take two or three coats of paint, but you will be able to cover the old paint.

Come-For-Tea Cloth and Napkins

Tea parties with friends are so much fun—especially when you use this cheery cherry set!

WHAT YOU'LL NEED

For the tea cloth

- Decorative-edged or straight scissors
- Small piece of white fabric or paper tablecloth
- Waxed paper
- Foam plate
- Red acrylic paint
- Knife
- Carrot
- Three shades of green crayons

For the napkins

- Waxed paper
- White paper napkins
- Paper doily
- Red paint pen or red felt-tip marker

HERE'S HOW
For the tea cloth

1 Cut the fabric to the size you want for the table, about 16x16 inches, rounding the corners if you wish.

2 Put waxed paper under the fabric. Spread some red paint on the plate. Have a grown-up help you cut a carrot in half, leaving a smooth cut.

▲**3** Carefully dip the carrot in the red paint and stamp the cloth using the circle. This will create cherry shapes. Cherries often grow in twos with a stem between. Stamp some of the circles like that. When you are happy with your stamping, let the paint dry.

▲**4** With the crayons, draw the leaves and the stems, mixing the colors as you go.

For the napkins

1 Put waxed paper on the table. Lay a white napkin on the paper and put the doily on top of the napkin.

▲**2** Keep the doily from slipping by holding it with one hand. Color over the doily lacy edge until it is covered with marker. Follow the edge of the doily with the marker to outline the shape. Pick up the doily to see the pretty pattern you have created. Repeat with the remaining napkins.

Best Friends Picture Frame

Make some new miniature friends! They look adorable perched on a plain picture frame that shows off your life-size pals.

WHAT YOU'LL NEED TO MAKE ONE DOLL

- Pencil
- Round top clothespin
- Acrylic paints
- Fine black permanent marker
- ⅛-inch wood wooden dowel
- Thick white crafts glue
- 5x7-inch acrylic flat frameless frame

HERE'S HOW

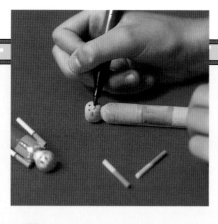

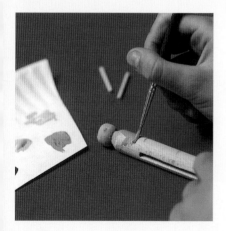

▲1 Using the photograph, *opposite*, and patterns, *right*, as guides, draw hair and clothes on the clothespin with a pencil.

▲2 Paint the hair and the clothes with acrylic paints in colors you like.

▲3 Use the black marker to draw the face, using one of the face patterns as a guide. Use the marker to draw legs and other small details as you like.

4 Paint the top of the arm dowels for sleeves and glue the dowels to each side of the clothespin. Make sure they are glued toward the front of the slit in the clothespin.

5 Insert your favorite picture in the acrylic frame. Put the frame together, clipping several clothespin friends at the top.

Awesome Paddleballs

Decoupage it! Paint it! Add dots galore!
Decorate your paddleball
to show off your personality!

WHAT YOU'LL NEED

- Purchased paddleball
- Acrylic paints
- Foam plate
- Paintbrush
- Pinking shears (zigzag scissors)
- Crafting foam
- Thick white crafts glue
- Plastic eyes; beads; buttons
- Greeting cards for decoupaging
- Decoupage medium

SNAP OUT OF IT

HERE'S HOW

For funny face paddleball

1 To add a funny face to your paddle, put a small amount of acrylic paint on a plate. Paint one side of the paddle. Let the paint dry. Turn the paddle over and paint the other side. Let the paint dry.

2 Using pinking shears, cut little narrow triangles from crafting foam. Glue the shapes to the paddle as shown.

▲ **3** Glue two eyes close together in the center of the paddle. Glue on a tiny bead for the nose and a round black button for the mouth.

4 Spread glue over the top of the handle. Sprinkle beads over the glue until the handle top is covered. Glue small dots of beads to the paddle if desired. Let the paddle dry overnight before using it.

For decoupaged paddleball

▲ **1** Paint your paddle however you wish. Let the paint dry thoroughly between coats. Add wavy stripes, dots, or any other designs. To make polka dots, dip a paintbrush handle into paint and touch it to the surface of the paddle. Let the paint dry thoroughly.

▲ **2** Cut out words or pictures from a favorite greeting card to glue onto your paddleball.

▼ **3** Spread decoupage medium on the back of the card and place it on the paddle. Glue on all of your cutouts and let the glue dry. Paint the entire paddle with decoupage medium again. (It may look white, but it will dry clear.) Let it dry.

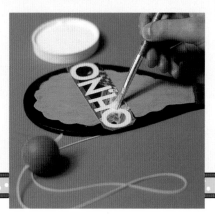

Pogo Stick Star

Hop to it—these pogo sticks will make you jump for joy!

WHAT YOU'LL NEED

- Scissors
- 2 yards each of two colors of ribbon
- Masking tape
- Pogo stick
- Thick white crafts glue
- Pencil
- Tracing paper
- Crafting foam in two colors
- Pinking shears (zigzag scissors)

HERE'S HOW

1 Cut a 50-inch-long piece from each color of ribbon.

2 With two of the ribbon ends even and laying side by side, tape the ribbons to one end of the pogo stick. Spread a line of glue a few inches long just below the tape.

3 Begin winding the ribbon around the stick covering the tape and glue. Keep winding the ribbon around the stick, adding more glue as you go.

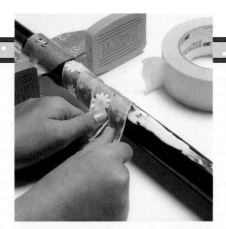

▲ **4** Trim any extra ribbon at the other end and tie a bow around the top. Trim the ribbon tails so they are the same length.

5 Trace the patterns, on *page 34 or 35*, onto tracing paper. Cut out the patterns and trace around them onto the crafting foam.

▲ **6** Cut out the shapes with pinking shears or straight-edged scissors. Bend the large star and cut two 1-inch slits in the center.

▲ **7** Pull the remaining piece of ribbon through the slits of the foam shape. Spread glue over the back of the small star and glue it on top of the large star, covering the slits and the ribbon. Tie the star to the pogo stick. Trim the ribbon ends if necessary.

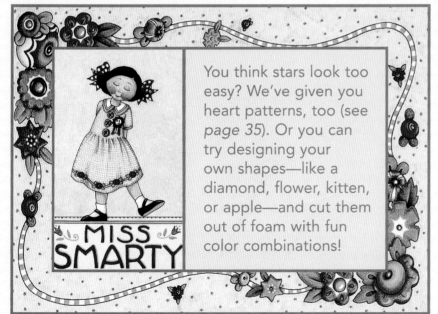

MISS SMARTY

You think stars look too easy? We've given you heart patterns, too (see *page 35*). Or you can try designing your own shapes—like a diamond, flower, kitten, or apple—and cut them out of foam with fun color combinations!

STAR PATTERNS

HEART PATTERNS

STEPPING OUT

From funky shoes to awesome barrettes,
you'll have a great time making really cool
things to wear. We'll show you how to
"glitter-up" a hat, string a colorful necklace—
even how to turn an ordinary umbrella
into one that makes people giggle! Turn
the page for some make-it, wear-it fun.

STEPPING OUT.

Silly Sneakers

You'll be the talk of the playground wearing these fanciful sneakers you can decoupage using Mary Engelbreit's artwork and a few painted dots!

WHAT YOU'LL NEED

- Mary Engelbreit wrapping paper or *Home Companion* magazines
- Scissors
- Paintbrush
- Decoupage medium
- Canvas tennis shoes
- Paint pens in colors you like

OH, NO

Q I put a cutout on my shoe but I want to move it! What do I do?

A As long as the decoupage medium is wet, carefully peel off the piece you want to move and place it somewhere else. If it's hard to peel, use a toothpick to lift a corner.

HERE'S HOW

1 Cut out wrapping paper motifs or the magazine drawings. Trim each piece carefully, removing all extra paper from around each design you like.

▲**2** With a paintbrush, brush a smooth coat of decoupage medium over the parts of the shoes where you want to add the cutouts. Let the shoes dry.

▶**3** Arrange the cutouts on the canvas areas of the shoes, putting decoupage medium under and over each piece.

4 After decoupage medium is dry, brush on three more coats, letting each dry before adding another coat.

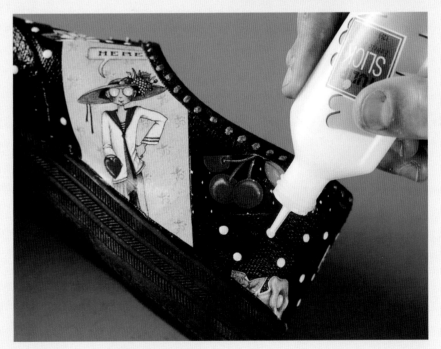

▲**5** After the shoes are dry, add dots of paint to the shoes wherever you wish.

Glitter Hats

You'll put sparkle in everyone's eyes with these fun-to-make caps that capture the glistening sun's rays!

WHAT YOU'LL NEED

- Waxed paper
- Decoupage medium
- Paintbrush
- Baseball-style cap
- Glitter or confetti
- Glitter gold fabric paint in a squirt bottle
- Jewels with flat back

HERE'S HOW

▼ **1** Cover your work surface with waxed paper. With a paintbrush, paint the entire bill of the cap with a thick coat of decoupage medium.

▼ **2** Sprinkle glitter or confetti onto the decoupage medium until the bill is covered well.

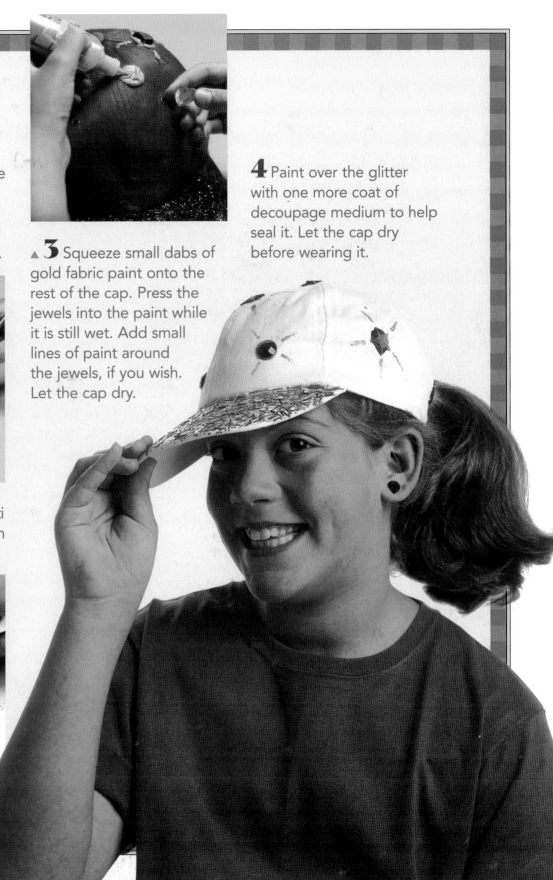

▲ **3** Squeeze small dabs of gold fabric paint onto the rest of the cap. Press the jewels into the paint while it is still wet. Add small lines of paint around the jewels, if you wish. Let the cap dry.

4 Paint over the glitter with one more coat of decoupage medium to help seal it. Let the cap dry before wearing it.

Fun (and funky) Barrettes

You'll be totally cool when you wear these barrettes made from the most

unexpected things you find around the house!

WHAT YOU'LL NEED

For sunglasses barrette
- Inexpensive sunglasses
- Tiny screwdriver, if needed
- Sandpaper
- Thick white crafts glue
- Assorted beads
- Fun-shaped buttons
- Barrette back

For comb barrette
- Small comb
- Sandpaper

- Embroidery floss and needle
- Assorted beads
- Thick white crafts glue
- Flower-shaped button
- Barrette back

For scissors barrette
- Small, blunt plastic scissors
- Sandpaper
- Curling ribbon
- Thick white crafts glue
- Barrette back

HERE'S HOW
For sunglasses barrette

▲ **1** Remove the sides of the sunglasses. Use a tiny screwdriver or pop them off.

▲ **2** Sand the back of the sunglasses slightly with the sandpaper to roughen the plastic. This will make the barrette back stick to the sunglasses better.

3 Glue beads and buttons across the top of the glasses. Let the glue dry. Glue the barrette back to the back of the sunglasses.

For comb barrette

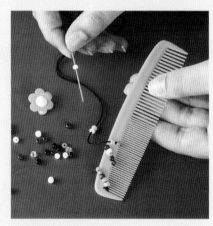

▲ **1** Sand the back of the comb slightly with sandpaper to roughen the plastic.

2 Thread the needle with three strands of embroidery floss. Tie the end of the floss tightly to one end of the comb. String beads onto the floss and wind around the comb between the teeth.

3 Clip the floss, leaving enough to tie at the other end. Tie the floss tightly.

4 Add small dabs of glue under the beads to make them stay. Glue the flower-shaped button to the teeth of the comb.

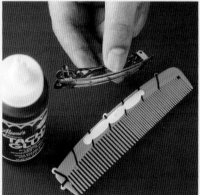

▲ **5** Glue the barrette back to the back of the comb.

Fun (and funky) Barrettes

For scissors barrette

1 Sand the back of the scissors (use only <u>blunt</u> scissors) slightly with sandpaper to roughen the plastic so the barrette back will stick better to the scissors. Sand the blade edges to dull them.

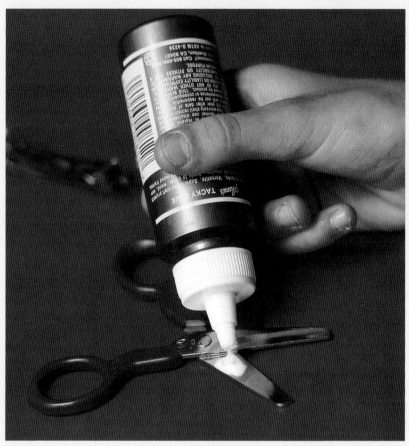

◄**2** Cut eight strands of curling ribbon and curl the ends.

▲**3** Open the scissors slightly and glue the blades so they stay apart.

◀ **4** Wind the ribbon between the blades and between the handles and glue in place. Let the glue dry. Glue the barrette back to one side of the scissors.

MISS SMARTY

So you have already made these three barrettes and it's only noon! Try gluing a barrette back to the back of a spoon, a playing card, or how about a fast-food kid's-meal toy? Use your imagination!

It's-Raining-Cats-and-Dogs Umbrella

It's raining, it's pouring but your umbrella won't be boring with Mary's lovable cats and dogs parading around the edge.

WHAT YOU'LL NEED

- Tracing paper or lightweight printer paper
- Pencil
- Scissors
- Clear tape
- An umbrella in a light color
- Fine-tip permanent black marker
- Paintbrush
- Acrylic paint in the colors you like

HERE'S HOW

1 Choose the cat or dog pictures you wish to draw on your umbrella by looking at the patterns on *pages 48-49*. Trace the patterns onto the tracing or printer paper. Cut them out leaving a little paper around the edges.

▲**2** Tape the patterns on the inside edge of the umbrella. You should be able to see the drawings through the umbrella fabric.

▶**3** Using the marker, trace the animal pictures. Continue drawing cats and dogs all around the edge of the umbrella. Write "it's raining cats and dogs" above the drawings.

4 Paint the top and tips of the umbrella using bright colors, if you wish. Let the paint dry.

IT'S-RAINING-CATS-AND-DOGS
UMBRELLA

Easy-As-Pie Necklaces

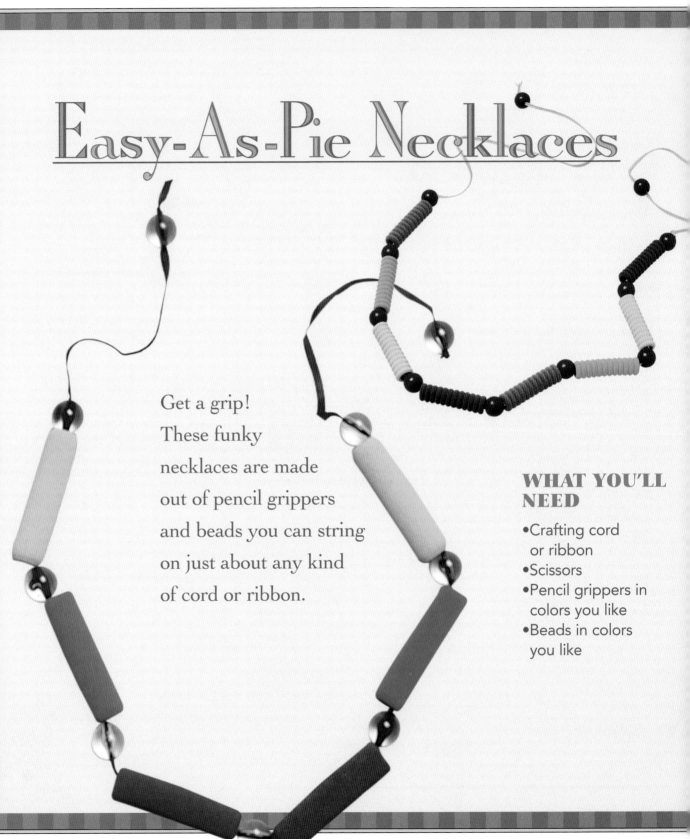

Get a grip!
These funky
necklaces are made
out of pencil grippers
and beads you can string
on just about any kind
of cord or ribbon.

WHAT YOU'LL NEED

- Crafting cord or ribbon
- Scissors
- Pencil grippers in colors you like
- Beads in colors you like

HERE'S HOW

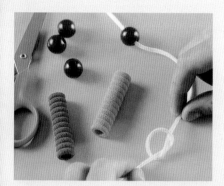

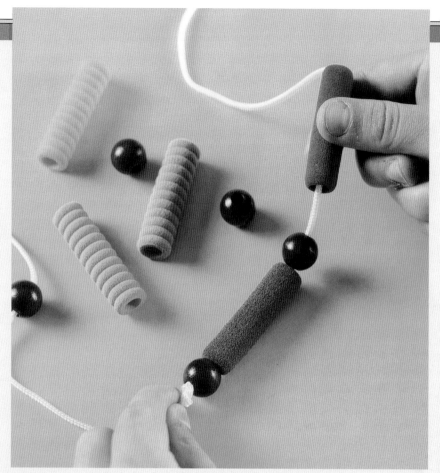

▲ **1** Decide how long you want the necklace. Cut a piece of cord 3 inches longer than the length you want your necklace. Tie a double knot at the end leaving about ½ inch.

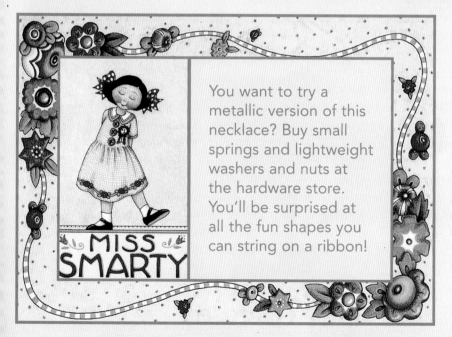

You want to try a metallic version of this necklace? Buy small springs and lightweight washers and nuts at the hardware store. You'll be surprised at all the fun shapes you can string on a ribbon!

MISS SMARTY

▲ **2** Thread a bead. Tie another double knot next to the bead. Tie another double knot about 3 inches from the first bead. Start threading the beads and grippers alternating beads and grippers until about 4 inches of cord remain.

3 Tie a double knot. Finish the end of the necklace the same way it was started.

Cuddle-Up Mittens

Your hands will stay toasty warm in these mittens and gloves that are so playful you won't ever want to take them off!

WHAT YOU'LL NEED

- Scissors
- Cardboard
- Gloves or mittens
- Needle and embroidery floss
- Thread to match gloves or mittens
- Sequins, beads, and buttons
- Fur trim

HERE'S HOW

1 Cut a piece of cardboard to fit into the palm of the glove or mitten. Slip it inside. (This will keep you from sewing your glove together.) To sew on buttons, beads, or sequins, first thread your needle with a thread to match your gloves. Use a double strand about 12 inches long. Knot the end.

2 Insert the needle where you want to attach a bead, button, or sequin. Catch the surface of the glove and sew a small stitch. Go over that same stitch two or three times so that it will hold. Trim the extra thread beyond the knot.

▶**3** String the bead onto the needle and insert the needle back into the glove. After the bead is sewed on, sew two or three more stitches in the glove fabric just to make sure it doesn't come off. You can also layer sequins and beads to get a fun look.

▼**4** If you want to sew a line, like on the mouths of the faces, use three strands of black embroidery floss, and sew stitches close together. Sew over them until you like how thick they look.

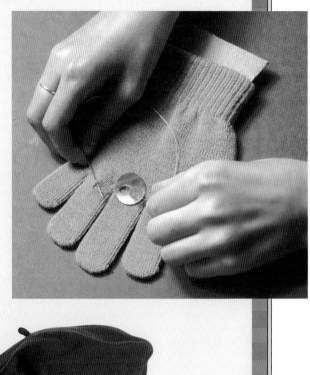

Earring Tree

A blast to make, wear, and put away—earrings have never been so much fun!

WHAT YOU'LL NEED

For the earrings
- Thick white crafts glue
- Buttons, paper clips, small appliqués, beads, wiggly eyes
- Earring backs
- Acrylic paint
- Disposable plastic plate
- Small ceramic tile
- Pencil with round-tip eraser
- Eraser topper in square shape

For the earring holder
- Picture frame
- Colored plastic canvas
- Pencil
- Scissors
- Thick white crafts glue

HERE'S HOW
For the earrings

▲ **1** Glue buttons, appliqués, beads, or paper clips to the earring backs using crafts glue. Allow to dry thoroughly before wearing.

▲ **2** For the tile earrings, put paint on a piece of plastic plate. Dip the round eraser end of the pencil in the paint and dab onto the tile for a flower center. Dip the square top eraser into the paint to make petals. Allow to dry. Glue an earring back to the tile. Let it dry.

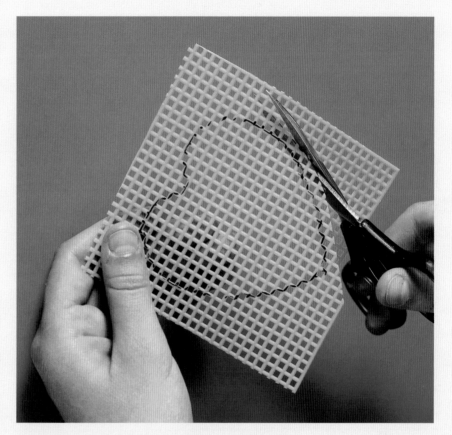

For the earring holder

▲ **1** Take the glass out of the picture frame. Lay the frame on the plastic canvas and draw around the inside of the frame. Use scissors to cut around the shape, leaving about ¼ inch all the way around the shape.

2 Glue the plastic canvas into the back of the frame using crafts glue. Let the glue dry.

3 Insert the pierced earring posts through the plastic canvas mesh and attach the earring backs to hold earrings in place.

ONE TOUCH OF NATURE

The wondrous, adventurous, tremendous OUTDOORS! How exciting it is to learn more about nature when you explore the world around you. This chapter shares crafts to make and games to play—all with the help and inspiration of Mother Nature.

ONE TOUCH of NATURE MAKES THE WHOLE WORLD KIN.

SHAKESPEARE

Stick-To-It Easel

This stick frame is so neat... don't be surprised if mom or dad wants you to make one for their desk!

WHAT YOU'LL NEED

For easel
- 4 sticks the same length, about 9 inches long
- Thick white crafts glue
- Embroidery floss in your favorite colors

For framed picture
- Your drawing or painting glued to cardboard
- 8 sticks about the same length to fit around picture
- Pliers or wire-cutter tool
- Embroidery floss in your favorite colors
- Thick white crafts glue

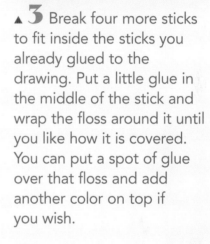

HERE'S HOW
For easel

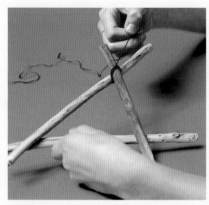

▲ **1** Make an "A" with three sticks. Use a little bit of glue to hold them together. Let the sticks set until they stay together. Carefully pick up the sticks and add more glue at the two bottom corners. Wrap the colored floss around and around the wet glue until you like how it looks.

▶ **2** After you have the two bottom corners done, add a little bit of glue to the back stick and place it against the other two. While holding it in place, wrap the colored floss around all three sticks at the top.

For frame

1 Begin with your drawing. If it's not drawn on cardboard, you can cut it out and glue it to a piece of cardboard.

2 Break off four straight sticks so they are all the same size as the edges of your cardboard. Have a grown-up help you if you need to use pliers or a wire-cutter tool. Glue the sticks to the edges of the cardboard.

▲ **3** Break four more sticks to fit inside the sticks you already glued to the drawing. Put a little glue in the middle of the stick and wrap the floss around it until you like how it is covered. You can put a spot of glue over that floss and add another color on top if you wish.

4 Glue the shorter sticks to the inside of the other sticks. Let the glue dry.

Outdoors Tic-Tac-Toe

Grab a friend and a shady spot to play this fun game
that you can make in a flash.

WHAT YOU'LL NEED

- Wood slice from a large tree (found or purchased)
- Damp rag
- Pencil or chalk
- Small twigs
- 4 small pebbles
- Thick white crafts glue
- Clear gloss spray, if you wish
- 2 different kinds of rocks for markers— 4 of each

HERE'S HOW

▼**1** Clean the wood slice with a damp rag. Use a pencil or piece of chalk to draw the tic-tac-toe grid onto the wood or put the pieces on the wood where you want them, breaking the twigs to fit.

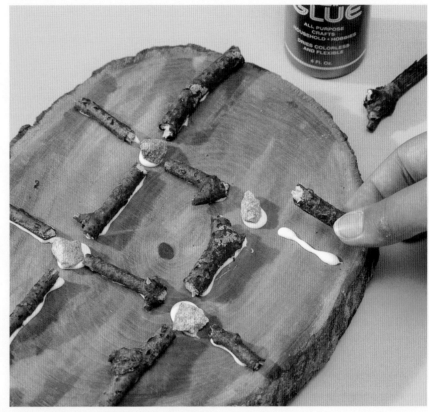

OH, NO

Q I can't find matching rocks to use as markers. What else can I use?

A Use acrylic paint to paint two sets of four matching rocks if you wish. Or, you can use four acorns and four small pinecones if you can't find enough stones to use.

▲**2** Glue the small pebbles and the twigs in place. Let the glue dry. If you wish, spray the entire piece with gloss spray.

3 Use the rocks for markers. Have fun...and good luck!

Stamp-It Picnic Tablecloth

Sponge colorful leaves around the edges of a tablecloth, then invite your best friends over for an outdoor tea party!

WHAT YOU'LL NEED

- Tracing paper
- Pencil
- Scissors
- Flat craft sponge (this is easy to cut and gets thick when you put it into water)
- Dish and water for soaking the sponge
- Waxed paper
- Acrylic paints or fabric paints
- Foam plate
- Purchased tablecloth

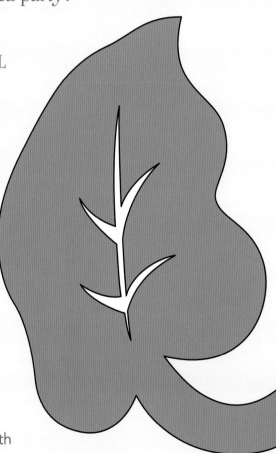

HERE'S HOW

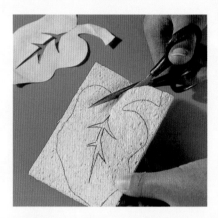

▲ **1** Lay the tracing paper over the leaf pattern, *left*, and trace around the outlines and veins. Cut out the pattern. Trace the leaf onto the sponge and cut it out. To cut the leaf veins, fold the leaf tip to the stem. Cut the long vein. Open the leaf up and cut the shorter veins. Soak the sponge in water and gently squeeze out the excess water.

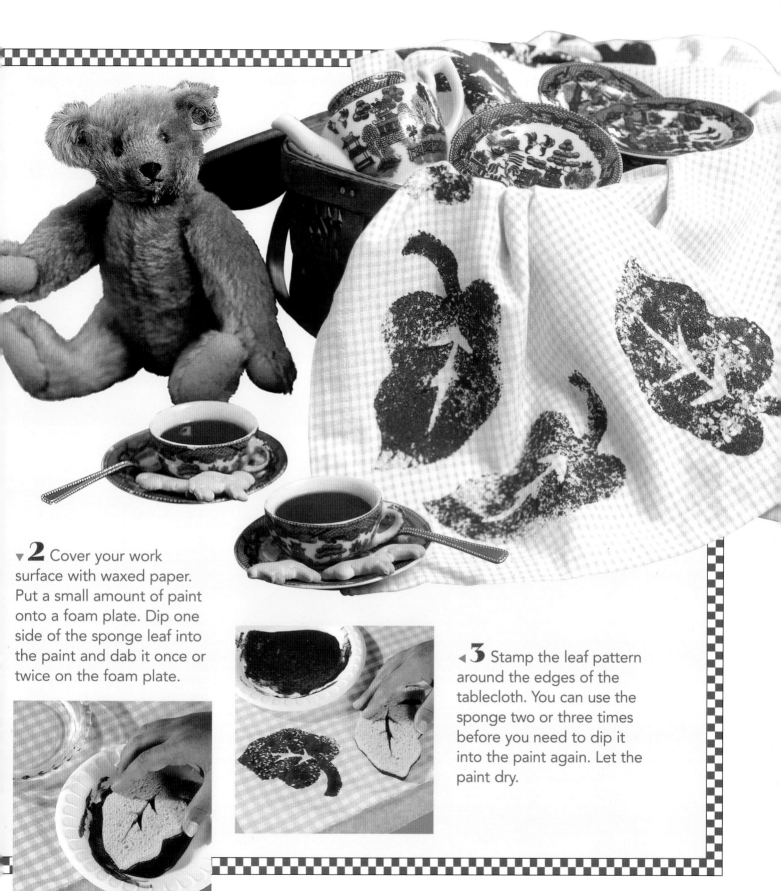

▼**2** Cover your work surface with waxed paper. Put a small amount of paint onto a foam plate. Dip one side of the sponge leaf into the paint and dab it once or twice on the foam plate.

◄**3** Stamp the leaf pattern around the edges of the tablecloth. You can use the sponge two or three times before you need to dip it into the paint again. Let the paint dry.

Bug Buddies

These little "creepy-crawlies" will wiggle
their way into your heart!

WHAT YOU'LL NEED

- Smooth rocks
- Items from nature like
  acorn caps, leaves, weeds,
  curly grapevine, sticks,
  corn, and pinecones
- Seeds (sunflower,
  pumpkin, or squash)

- Acrylic paints; paintbrush
- Foam plate
- Thick white crafts glue

HERE'S HOW

▲ **1** Gather rocks and other
nature items to add
character to your bugs.
Wash and dry the rocks.

2 Lay the rocks and other nature items out and decide how you will put them together. (Look at the photos on *pages 64* and *66–67* for ideas.) Using a generous amount of glue, glue the rocks together however you want them arranged. Let the glue dry an hour or two.

3 Put a small amount of paint on the plate and paint the rocks and nature items in colors you like. Let the paint

MISS SMARTY

These rock bugs are too easy to paint? Try making a set of people that looks like your family or close friends. You can even make clothes and hats using felt scraps. To add glasses, just bend wire to fit the face shape.

dry. You can add stripes or dots to your bugs. To make stripes, use a thin pointed paintbrush, dip it in paint, and slowly draw a neat line. To make dots, dip the handle end of the brush in the paint, and dot it on to the rock. Let the paint dry.

4 Glue the nature items to the rock bodies. *To make antennas*, use a piece of grass, weed, or grapevine.

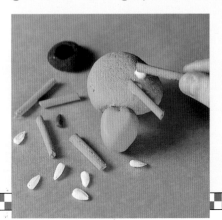

To make hats, use acorn caps. *To make noses, hands, and feet*, use seeds. *To make arms and legs*, cut small sections from sticks. *To make a bee's crown*, peel off tiny petals from a pine cone. *To make wings*, use leaves (the paint will stick better if they are a little dry).

5 To make the eyes, paint the white part first. Dip the handle end of a paintbrush into white paint and dot it on the rock. Let the paint dry. To make a black dot, dip a smaller paintbrush handle into paint and dot on the white dot. Paint eyelids on top of the eyes if you wish.

Bradley Beetle

Beth Butterfly

Lucy Ladybug

Harry Hornet

BUG BUDDIES

Carrie Caterpillar

Freddy Fly

George Grasshopper

Bea Bumblebee

Leaf-It-To-Nature Frame

Take a nature walk and gather a handful of clover and interesting shaped leaves to make an out-of-this-world picture frame.

WHAT YOU'LL NEED

- Clovers, leaves, ferns, or other flat fresh greenery
- Picture frame and two mats
- Scissors
- Decoupage medium
- Paintbrush
- Picture or drawing

HERE'S HOW

▲ **1** Decide how you would like the greenery arranged on the mats and frame, trimming the pieces if needed.

▲ **2** Starting with the frame, cover the entire front and sides with decoupage medium. Place the greenery on the frame, pressing the pieces into place.

▲ **3** When all the pieces are arranged on the frame, add two more coats of decoupage medium, letting it dry between coats.

4 Decoupage greenery onto the mats the same way as you did for the frame. Let all of the decoupage medium dry. Tape a drawing or photograph in place behind the mats and put the drawing into the frame.

MISS SMARTY

You've found lots of neat greenery, but your mat and frame are finished? Try decoupaging your nature finds in the corner of stationery, on the front cover of a school folder, or on an "I love you" card for your mom and dad.

THE PRINCESS OF QUITE-A-LOT

Dress up in a costume you've made! Look like a princess or a flower in the shade! It's fun to play make-believe, and we'll share some crafting ideas to help make pretend time a blast—with things to wear on top of your head, over your shoulders, and even on your toes!

Queen-For-A-Day Costume

Everyone will treat you like royalty when you dress the part!

WHAT YOU'LL NEED

For the cape
- 1⅛ yards of 45-inch-wide purple felt
- Old magazine
- Thumbtack; chalk
- 20-inch-long piece of string
- Tape
- Tracing paper
- Scissors
- Thick white crafts glue
- 2½ yards of fur trim

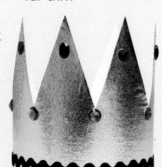

HERE'S HOW
For cape

2 Trace the circle neck pattern, *page 77*, onto the tracing paper. Center it over the felt circle, matching the dot on the pattern to the tack. Cut out both circles.

▲**3** To add the fur trim, put glue on the back of the fur trim and spread it around well to cover it all. Start by gluing it to the edge of the cape. If it is difficult to glue around the curves, make a small clip, about ½ inch, in the edge of the fur. Let the glue dry.

▲**1** To cut a circle from the felt, lay the felt flat on a big surface. Put an old magazine under the center of the felt. Stick a thumbtack in the middle of the felt. Wind an end of the string around the chalk and tape it tightly, then take the other end of the string and wind it tightly around the thumbtack. Hold the chalk out from the center as in the picture and draw your circle (see the drawing on *page 76*). You may need someone to help hold the tack still.

WHAT YOU'LL NEED

For crown

- Scissors
- Poster board
- Gold vinyl (in the upholstery section of a fabric store)
- Thick white crafts glue
- Tape measure
- Tracing paper
- Pencil
- 26 inches of black wide rickrack
- Rhinestones
- Self-adhesive Velcro®

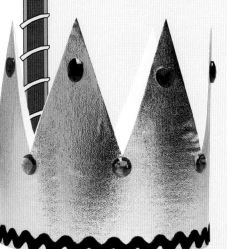

WHAT YOU'LL NEED

For scepter

- Blue acrylic paint
- Paintbrush, foam plate, and water
- 36-inch piece of ½ inch wooden dowel
- 5-inch Styrofoam ball
- 18-inch-square piece of red Mylar
- 10 inches of string
- Plastic-head straight pins
- 1 yard of gold braid, cut in half
- Strong tape
- Thick white crafts glue
- ¼- and ½-inch-wide gold ribbons
- Scissors; black and white beads
- 6-inch-long piece of wire

HERE'S HOW
For crown

1 Cut an 8x26-inch piece from the poster board and the vinyl. Glue the pieces together and set aside.

▼ **2** To make a pattern, measure around your head where the crown will go and add 4 inches. Cut a 3-inch-high piece of tracing paper to this length.

Trace the triangle pattern, *page 76*, on tracing paper and cut enough triangles to fit on top of the rectangle, leaving a little space on both ends. Tape the pieces together. Trace your pattern onto the back of the poster board with the vinyl glued to it. Cut out the crown shape.

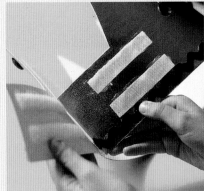

◄ **3** Glue on rickrack and rhinestones. Add the Velcro. Try on the crown so you know where to put the Velcro pieces. One Velcro piece should go on the gold part and the other should go on the back side of the vinyl.

HERE'S HOW
For scepter

1 Put a small amount of paint on a plate and paint the stick blue. Let it dry. Push the stick into center of Styrofoam ball.

▲2 Wrap the Mylar around the ball, twist tightly at the bottom, and tie with string. Trim off the extra Mylar.

3 Put a straight pin in the center of an 18-inch piece of braid and pin it to the top of the ball. Take the other 18-inch piece of braid and pin it in the same place but make it cross the other braid. Bring both ends to the bottom and pin them. Let the extra braid hang down.

▲4 Cover the ends of the braid and Mylar by wrapping tape tightly to secure it.

▼5 To hide the tape, cover it with glue, and wrap ¼-inch-wide gold ribbon around the tape.

▲6 Glue ½-inch-wide gold ribbon on dowel, winding as you go. Trim off extra ribbon.

7 Decorate the top of the ball with straight pins and beads. Put a wire through the top bead, bring the ends of the wire together and push through the other beads. Add a dot of glue and push into the ball.

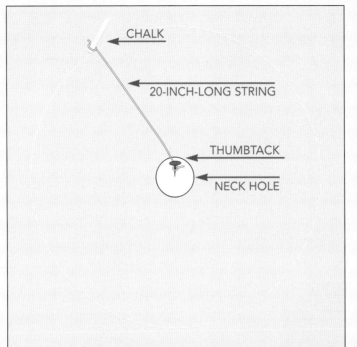

HOW TO MAKE THE CIRCLE FOR YOUR CAPE

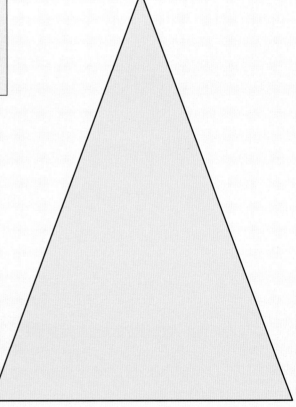

CROWN POINT

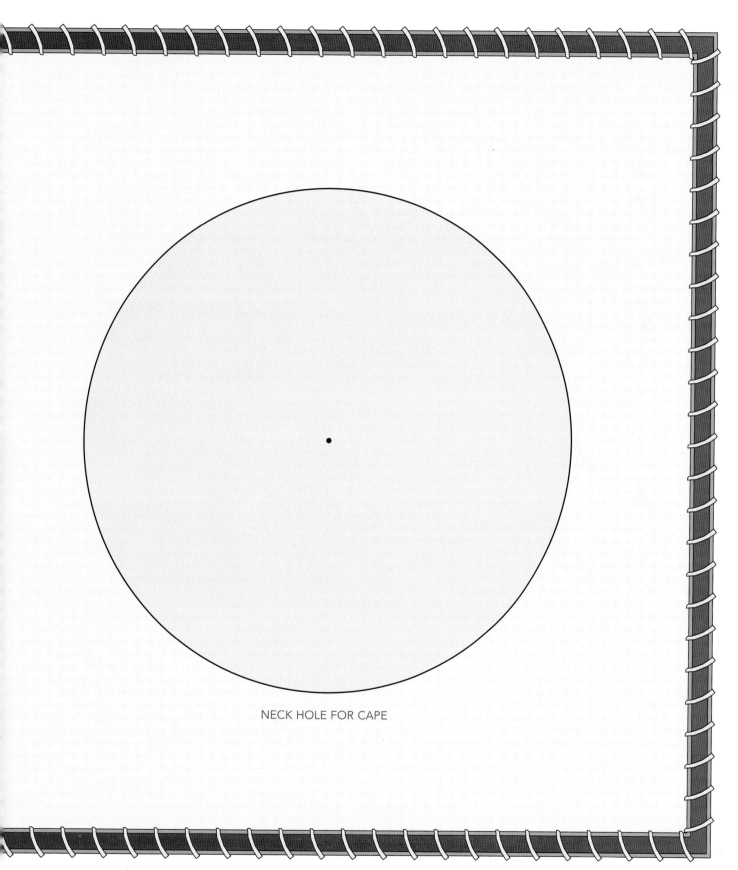

NECK HOLE FOR CAPE

Hilarious Heels and Satchels

Get glamorous when you slip on these oh-so-fancy shoes and purses you decorate using everything from fluffy feathers to sparkling gems!

WHAT YOU'LL NEED

- Adult-size pump-style shoes; purse
- Paint pen in colors you like
- Thick white crafts glue
- Buttons, gems, feathers, and pom-poms in various sizes and colors

HERE'S HOW

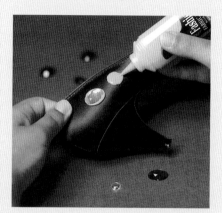

▲ **1** To dress up your shoes or purse with gems or buttons, use paint pen to make a circle of paint, about the size of the gem or button.

▲ **2** Gently push the trim into the paint pen, letting the paint cover the edges of the trim and oozing through any holes in buttons. Once the paint begins to set, you can layer buttons by using more paint to hold them together.

3 To add feathers or pom-poms, use dots of crafts glue to stick them to the purse or shoes.

MISS SMARTY

You've trimmed one side of a purse and want to do more? Let the first side dry completely and turn the purse over. Write the names of all of your friends on the other side. Let the paint dry.

My Own Dress-Up Suitcase

Dress up an old suitcase to keep all your garb for make-believe time handy and easy to find.

WHAT YOU'LL NEED

- Old suitcase
- Fine sandpaper, if needed
- Pink and black acrylic paints
- Bowl; water
- Paintbrushes
- Dish soap
- Vinyl metallic letter stickers
- Hologram stickers
- Soft dry cloth
- Hologram sticker paper
- Decorative-edged scissors
- Little mirrors
- String of sequins

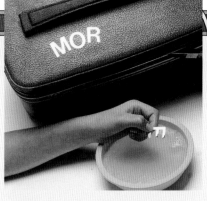

HERE'S HOW

1 If necessary, clean and dry the outside of the suitcase. If it has a very slick surface, sand it with fine sandpaper to make the paint adhere better.

▲**2** Paint the light pink areas first. You don't have to be extremely careful. The pink paint can be covered by the black paint later. Let the paint dry. Paint on a second coat of pink, if needed, and let it dry.

3 Paint all the black areas, painting neatly on the edges next to the pink. Paint the handle too. Let it dry.

▲**4** To begin decorating with the permanent vinyl stickers, first mix a drop or two of dish soap into a cereal bowl filled with water. Take the letters off the backing one at a time and dip them into the soapy water. They will be slippery and dripping wet. Place them onto the suitcase. (Your letters don't have to be perfectly straight. After you put them on, you'll have plenty of time to move them around until you like how they are placed.) When you are happy with where

they are, dab off the extra water with a soft dry cloth. The letters will dry and stick well within a few hours.

▶**5** To add more trims, use hologram sticker paper cut into shapes. Cut squiggly petal shapes, leaves, lines, or other shapes by using decorative-edged scissors. Glue on little mirrors where you would like them. Squirt on a line of glue to add a string of sequins.

OH, NO

Q You dropped your paintbrush and got black on the pink paint?

A Don't worry! Cover up your "oops" by gluing a mirror or other trim you like over your mistake. Or, if it is still wet, wipe it off and repaint the area with the pink paint.

Petal Heads

Wear these simply silly hats for play
or as a topper for a one-of-a-kind
Halloween costume!

WHAT YOU'LL NEED

- 18-inch-wide brim straw hat
- Yellow acrylic paint
- Green acrylic paint
- Paintbrush, water, and foam plate
- Tracing paper and pencil
- Scissors
- ¼ yard of upholstery vinyl in a color you like
- Thick white crafts glue
- ¾ yard of green pom-pom upholstery trim

HERE'S HOW

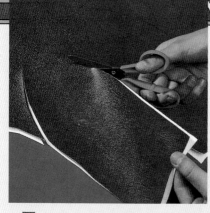

▲**1** Paint the top part of the hat yellow. Let it dry. Paint the under side of the brim green. You do not have to paint inside where it fits onto your head. Let the paint dry.

▼**2** Make a petal pattern by tracing a pattern, *pages 84–85*, onto tracing paper. Cut out the pattern. Lay the piece of vinyl flat and trace around the pattern. (You will need about 16 pointed petals or 24 rounded petals.)

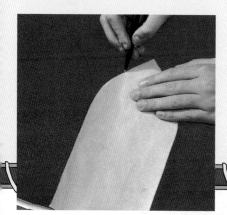

▲**3** To save time, you can fold the vinyl in half and cut two petals at once.

▲**4** Lay the petals onto the hat brim and spread them around so they look even. Overlap one petal on top of the other as in the picture. Glue each petal onto the hat with crafts glue, and press it down. Work around the hat until all the petals are on.

▲**5** Squeeze a line of glue onto the hat where the green pom-pom trim will be attached. Press the trim onto the hat and cut off any extra.

POINTED PETAL PATTERN

ROUNDED PETAL PATTERN

Princess Tiara

You'll want to wave like a beauty queen when you wear this sparkling crown.

WHAT YOU'LL NEED

- Tracing paper; pencil; scissors
- Sheet of white crafting foam
- Cloth-covered plastic headband
- Thick white crafts glue
- 2 yards of ¼-inch-wide white satin ribbon; piece of paper
- Silver glitter
- 20-inch-long string of sequins
- Round and star-shaped rhinestones

HERE'S HOW

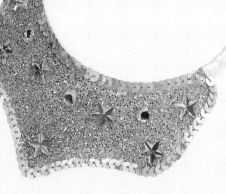

▲ **1** Choose the pattern you like, *pages 88–89*, and trace it onto tracing paper. (We've given you a crown tiara and a scalloped tiara pattern.) Cut it out and trace around the pattern onto the white foam. Cut out the tiara shape.

▶ **2** Spread plenty of crafts glue along the foam, from a notch to the end. Place the foam shape on the headband, keeping it centered. Wrap thin white ribbon around the glued section and tie it to hold it securely. You now have one side attached.

3 Glue the middle section of the tiara to the headband. Then glue the other side and tie with a ribbon as you did for the first side.

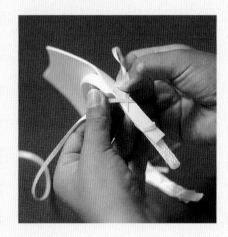

▲ **4** Place the tiara on a piece of paper and cover the tiara with glue where you want to add glitter. Spread glue to the edges. Place a string of sequins along the edge to outline it. Fill in the inside with silver glitter, sprinkling it heavily and shaking it off onto paper to put back in the bottle.

5 To add jewels, put a dab of glue on top of the glitter and press the rhinestones into the glue. Let the glue dry.

6 Cover the ends of ribbon with a thin coat of glue and wrap around until the entire side of the headband is covered with ribbon.

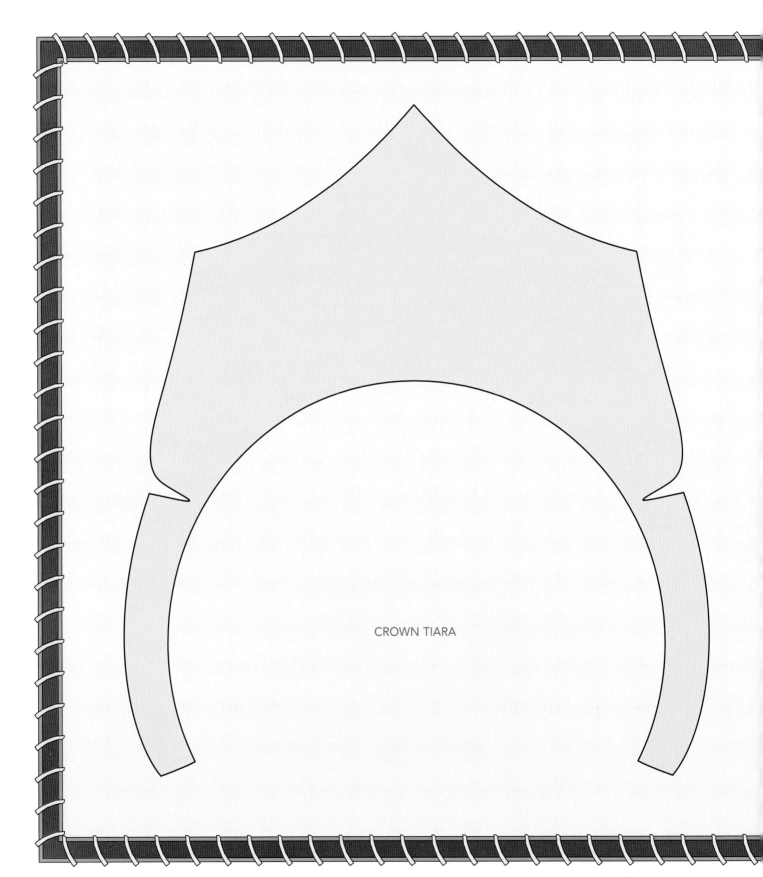

CROWN TIARA

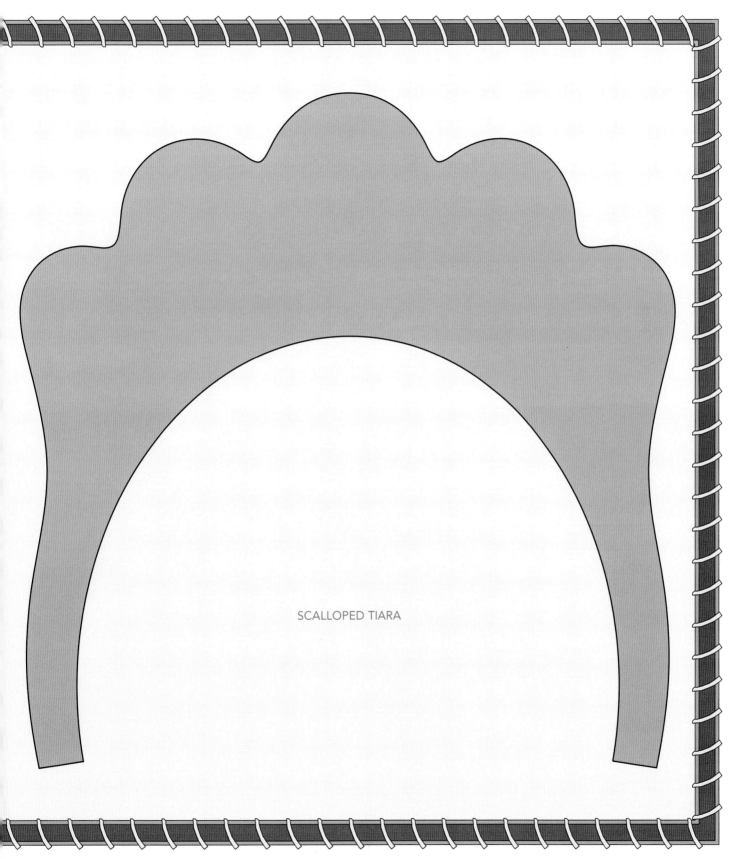

SCALLOPED TIARA

Victorian Headpiece

Pretend you're the damsel in distress with this dainty headpiece that's as pretty as those worn long ago.

WHAT YOU'LL NEED

- 3 colors of bridal tulle or netting, like purple, orange, and red, or any colors you like (½ yard each of 72-inch-wide tulle)
- Two small rubber bands
- Tape
- Thick white crafts glue
- Satin ribbon flowers

HERE'S HOW

▲1 Hold the three strands of tulle together and secure one end with a rubber band. Tape the end to a firm surface.

▼2 Braid the three strands of tulle together. Put another rubber band on the other end to hold it. Now you have a braided piece with a rubber band on each end.

▼3 Holding an end of the braid in each hand, place the center of the braid on the center of your forehead, bring the braid around to the

back of your head and knot it in the back. Take it off your head. Take off the rubber bands and undo the braid just up to the knot.

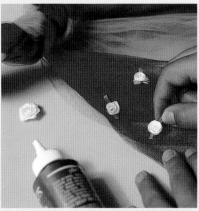

▲4 Glue satin ribbon flowers to the braid and the veil. Let the glue dry overnight before wearing the veil.

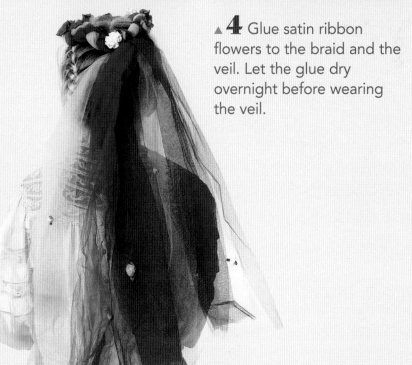

WELL, AIN'T YOU SOMETHIN'?!

Get ready (grab your crafting stuff)...get set (find a quiet spot)...go (create really cool gifts and more—all by yourself)! It's easy to make neat things to be proud of and to share with your family and friends. Just peek through this chapter and see!

Sticker Stationery

Go sticker crazy making this clever stationery— it's so easy, you'll want to make some for your friends!

WHAT YOU'LL NEED

- 8½x11-inch sheets of paper in colors you like
- Scissors
- 1x3-inch white labels
- Round stickers in a variety of colors
- Black and green marking pens
- Colored and white self-adhesive notebook paper reinforcements

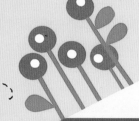

HERE'S HOW
For white picket fence stationery

▲**1** Cut three 1x3-inch labels in half, cutting the length of the label to make a fencepost. Cut points on one end of five fence posts.

2 Starting with the fence posts, stick them to the paper, making sure the points are facing up. Stick the fence posts on the paper, with all the bottom edges even and spaced about ¼ inch apart. Cut the remaining strip in half and press them on top of the fence posts as shown.

3 Add flowers in front of the fence as you wish, using various sizes of round stickers.

▼**4** To make leaves, cut the shape from a large round green sticker.

For butterfly stationery

1 To make the butterfly, cut a round sticker in half. Peel off the backing and press on the paper where you want your butterfly. Peel off the other half of the round sticker and place it next to the first, putting the rounded edges together. Cut a V-shaped piece from a label for the antennae, adding small round stickers to each point.

2 Add flowers to the bottom of the stationery as you did for the white picket fence stationery. Cut narrow strips from green labels for the stems.

3 Using a marking pen, draw dotted lines below the butterfly as shown in the photograph, *opposite*.

For polka–dot stationery

1 Pick the colors of round stickers and reinforcements you wish to use.

2 Press on the round stickers first, sticking them on the outer edges of the piece of paper. If some go off the edge of the paper, trim off with scissors.

3 Fill in with notebook paper reinforcements, pressing some on top of the round stickers. Be sure to leave a blank space in the middle to write a letter!

Pretty Pasta Ornaments

Colors and shapes and sizes—
oh, my! These pasta pretties are
so much fun to make, you'll want
to share the idea with your friends!

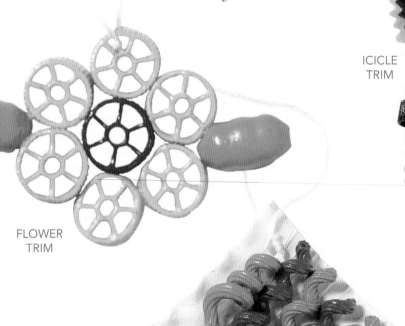

FLOWER
TRIM

ICICLE
TRIM

TWIRLY
TRIM

See more trims on pages 98–99.

WHAT YOU'LL NEED

- Any fun-shaped pasta like lasagna spaghetti, alphabets, shells, rotini, rigatoni, couscous, wheels, and
- Water, bowl
- Scissors
- Short drinking straw
- Paper towels
- Paintbrushes
- Foam plate
- Blue, red, yellow, purple, black, green, white, and pink acrylic paints
- Thick white crafts glue
- Fine string or embroidery floss

HERE'S HOW

▲ **1** To make lasagna-backed ornaments, soak the lasagna in a bowl of warm water just long enough to soften it so you can cut it with scissors without splitting it. This will take about 30 to 40 minutes. Don't let it soak too long or it

will get mushy. Make a hole with a straw for hanging. Blot excess water with paper towels and allow the lasagna to dry.

◄ **2** Paint pasta pieces in colors you like. When painting a lot of tiny pieces such as the couscous or alphabet macaroni, put the pieces on a foam plate and paint them in a pile and let it dry. Be careful not to use too much paint.

3 If using lasagna, glue the pieces on it however you wish. For other styles of ornaments, glue the pieces together or string them on fine string or embroidery floss if they have holes in the centers. Look at *pages 96* and *98–99* for ideas. Allow the trims to dry.

4 Tie a piece of string at the top of each ornament for hanging.

MISS SMARTY

You've made pasta ornaments for all of your friends and want to personalize them? Use alphabet macaroni to spell out names, special phrases, or sweet sentiments on the trims and paint them to match the trim.

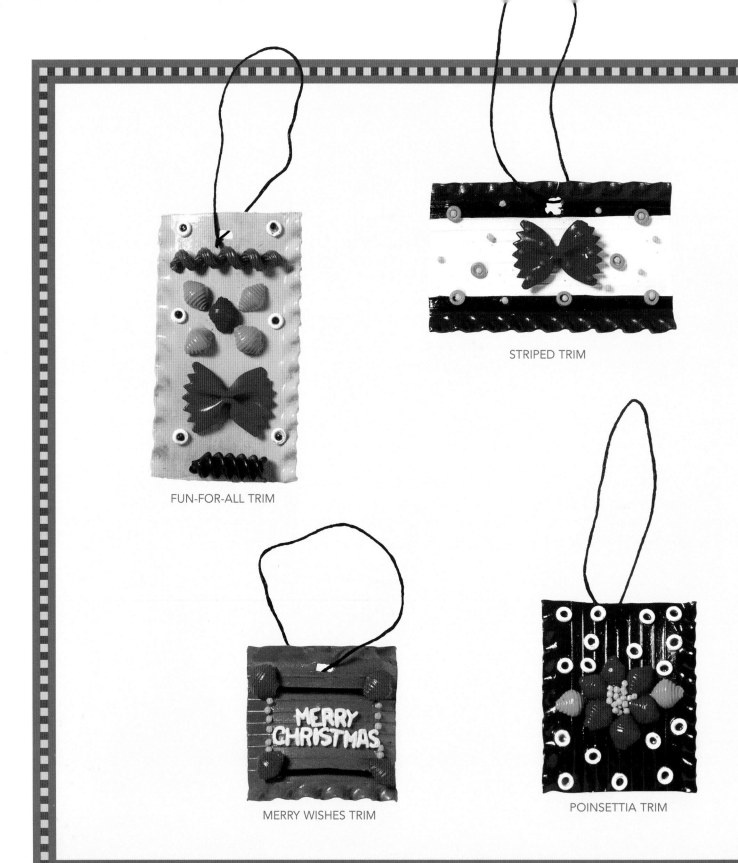

FUN-FOR-ALL TRIM

STRIPED TRIM

MERRY WISHES TRIM

POINSETTIA TRIM

BOW-TIE TRIM

'ROUND AND 'ROUND TRIM

POLKA-DOT TRIM

TIED-UP-TIGHT TRIM

Petal Pusher Candles

Add fun blooms to plain candles by
pressing tacks and pins into a candle.

WHAT YOU'LL NEED

- Pillar candle in a
  size and color
  you like

- Push-pins,
  map pins,
  or thumbtacks

HERE'S HOW

1 Remove wrapping from the candle.

▶ 2 Push a pin or tack into the candle. This will be a flower center. Choose another color of pin or tack to make a petal. Push it into the candle around the pin you used for the center of the flower.

▶ 3 Push in petals until the center is surrounded.

4 Keep making flower designs, spacing flowers as far apart as you wish. If you want to add stems, use green map pins. You can make flowers all around the candle or only on one side.

5 Put the candle in a candleholder and ask a grown-up to light your candle for everyone to enjoy.

My Own Special Scrapbook

Protect your book of memories with a cover you design with your own favorite drawings.

MY SCRAPBOOK

WHAT YOU'LL NEED

- Newspapers
- Scissors
- Your own drawings or artwork
- Scrapbook
- Purple acrylic paint or any color you like
- Foam plate
- Paintbrush
- Decoupage medium
- Yellow fabric paint in a squirt bottle (or any color you like)

HERE'S HOW

1 Cover your work surface with newspapers. Cut out your drawings. Put them on the scrapbook cover and decide how you want them arranged.

▲**2** Put some acrylic paint on a foam plate. Paint the entire cover of your scrapbook. Let it dry. (If it looks streaky, you can apply another coat of paint.) Clean your brush very well in water. Let the paint dry.

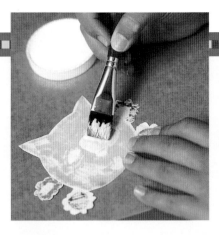

▲**3** Pour some decoupage medium into the lid. Using a paintbrush, coat the back of your drawing with decoupage medium. Cover the whole piece of paper well. Before the decoupage medium dries, turn the artwork over and put it on your book cover where you want it placed. To smooth out any wrinkles, press them down firmly using the paintbrush. Finish decoupaging all of your drawings this way.

▲**4** When the drawings feel dry to the touch, paint the entire scrapbook cover with decoupage medium. (It might look white, but it will dry clear.) Using a bottle of yellow fabric paint, write "MY SCRAPBOOK" or anything you wish. (It is best to write your letters in pencil first. If you make a mistake with a pencil, it will wipe off with a wet napkin.) You can outline your pictures or make lines, dots, or squiggles.

OH, NO

Q Can I put a drawing that I made with washable markers on my scrapbook?

A No. Drawings made using washable markers might smear when you decoupage them. Instead, use drawings made from crayons, colored pencil, paints, and permanent markers.

Year-Round Greeting Cards

Let someone know how special you think they are with a cheerful greeting card that's made by you... especially for them!

WHAT YOU'LL NEED

- Tracing paper
- Pencil
- Scissors—straight, decorative-edged, and pinking shears
- Wrapping paper or decorative papers like those used for memory books
- Colored card paper
- Glue stick
- Markers and paint pens
- Fabric paint
- Envelopes to fit cards
- Paper doilies

HERE'S HOW

Choose the paper you want to use to make a card. Fold it in half and cut it in a square or rectangular shape to fit inside the envelope.

For birthday card

1 Trace the patterns, *page 107*, onto tracing paper and cut them out.

2 Trace around the candle patterns on the decorative paper as many times as you wish. Glue the candles onto the front of the card.

3 For each candle flame, trace around the pattern on yellow paper. Cut out the flame shapes and glue them above the candles. Write a message using a paint pen.

For Easter card

1 Cut a rectangle slightly smaller than the folded card, using decorative-edged or straight scissors.

2 Trace the patterns on *page 106* and cut out. Trace around the patterns on the papers you like and cut out. Cut fringes in the top of the grass shape.

3 Glue the pieces in place as shown, *opposite*. Glue the beak to the head, and the head to the body. *Do not* glue the chick to the card. Glue *only* the bottom edge of the egg (so the chick can slip in and out).

For Christmas card

1 Cut rectangles from white paper. With paint pen, write "Merry Christmas" on the paper in various languages (Feliz Navidad is Spanish, Mele Kalikimaka is Hawaiian, and Joyeux Noel is French).

2 Let the paint dry. Glue the messages onto the card where you wish. Outline the rectangles using paint pen.

For Valentine's Day card

1 Write "I Love You" with bright red fabric paint on a white doily. Let the paint dry.

2 Glue the doily on the front of the card and let the glue dry.

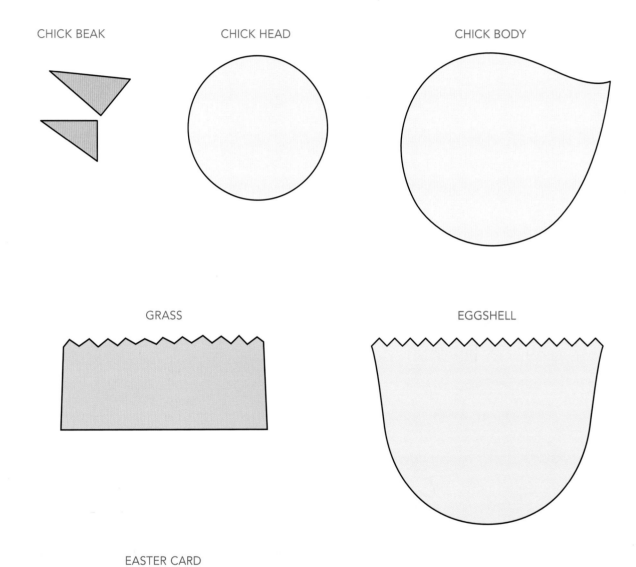

CHICK BEAK

CHICK HEAD

CHICK BODY

GRASS

EGGSHELL

EASTER CARD

HAPPY BIRTHDAY CARD

Clean-Up Queen

Make a mess when you play—it's okay!
Because now you can clean it up yourself with
this dazzling duo!

WHAT YOU'LL NEED

- Cup, water, and dish soap
- Vinyl letters
- Dustpan and brush
- Thick white crafts glue
- Strand of sequins
- Gold glitter
- Jewels; scissors

HERE'S HOW

▲ **1** To adhere the letters, first fill a cup with water and add a couple drops of dish soap. Remove the letters from their package, dip them in the soapy water and place on the dustpan. They

will be slippery and can be moved around. Move them until you like how they are positioned (they do not have to be perfectly straight). They will stick permanently after a few hours.

◄ **2** Glue the strand of sequins around the edge of the dustpan.

◄ **3** Cover the back of the brush handle with glue. Spread it around evenly and generously. Outline the edge with a string of sequins first. Sprinkle glitter onto the wet glue inside the sequins and gently shake the extra glitter off onto a newspaper. Let the glue dry. Glue jewels where you would like them. Let the glue dry for at least a day before using the set.

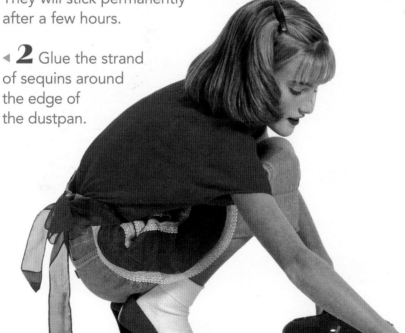

Dear Parents:

Is this a book to keep little hands busy on a rainy day? A learning tool? An idea book to inspire children's creativity? YES! This oh-so-fun crafts book for kids ages 6–14 is all that and more.

THE CRAFTS

From dress-me-up shoes and make-believe tiaras to tied-up-tight twig frames and decorated rocks that are literally as cute as a bug, the projects in this book are loved by kids.

For the majority of the crafts, once the supplies are on hand, you can turn your child loose to create his or her works of art and whimsy. And don't be surprised when your child nearly explodes proudly boasting, "I made it all by myself!"

Of course, it's always fun to craft together. Sharing time together while your child experiences the creative process can be a whole lot of fun for everyone.

MISS SMARTY

Do you have an ambitious child who likes a challenge? Throughout the book we've included Miss Smartys — suggestions for taking a project one step further. This opens a child's mind to options, inspires the imagination, and encourages discovery!

OH, NO!

Children are bound to find obstacles in the crafting process, such as making a mistake or not having the supplies as listed for a project. We'll let them know…it's okay! Some commonly faced problems are addressed and resolved so the child feels more confident and ultimately finds success and self-satisfaction.

THE TOOLS

Gathering supplies is a learning lesson in itself. You could purchase the materials for your child, but it's even more fun when they help! After they've chosen a project they want to make, have them write a list of the supplies they'll need to buy. Take them to a crafts or discount store where they can find the items. From this simple experience, they'll learn how to follow directions, how to choose materials and compare prices, and how to make substitutions when necessary.

If you'd like to start your child with a basic crafter's tool kit, we suggest the following supplies:
- Thick white crafts glue
- Waxed paper
- Scissors (both straight edged and decorative-edged types)
- Ruler
- Pencils with erasers
- Marking pens
- Acrylic paints
- Paintbrushes
- An old shirt or smock (decorating it with fabric paints is a fun project in itself!)

Have your child think up a container to keep the crafts supplies in. Maybe it will be a hat box, a tool box, or a shoe box—whatever it is, your child can decorate it using the techniques learned in this book!

So turn your child's creative imagination loose and feel good about encouraging his or her artistic flair. The process is so educational and better yet…A WHOLE LOT OF FUN!